Healthy Dips

40 Low Carb, Vegetarian and Vegan Dips and Dippers for Perfect Party Snacks

Copyright Notice

Reproduction, duplication, transmission of this document in part or in whole is permitted only with written permission from the publisher. All rights reserved.

Respective brands and trademarks mentioned in this book belong to their respective owners.

Disclaimer

This document is geared towards providing summarization of information related to the topic. While all attempts have been made to verify the accuracy of the information, the author does not assume any responsibility for errors, omissions, or interpretations of the content. The information is offered for informational or entertainment purposes only. If professional advice is necessary, a qualified legal, medical, financial or another respective professional should be consulted. **The reader is responsible for his or her own actions. The publisher does not accept any responsibility or liability arising from damages or losses, real or perceived, direct or indirect, resulting from the use of this information.**

Table of Contents

Author's Foreword 9

Chapter One: Creating Healthy and Fun Dips For Parties 14

    Picking the Dip 14

    Making the Perfect Party Dip 15

    What are the Best Dippers for Dips? 18

Chapter Two: Vegan and Vegetarian-Friendly Dips 21

    Best Vegan Dips for Parties 21

    Baba Ghanoush Dip/Spread 21

    Tzatziki 23

    Artichoke Hearts 25

    Onion Dip 28

    Carrot Hummus 30

    Vegetarian Dips Everyone Will Love 32

    Red Bell Pepper Dip 32

    Dill Dip 34

    Cheese and Herb Dip 36

Edamame Dip...38

Roasted Pumpkin Dip...40

Chapter Three: Authentic Inspired Dips Turned Low Carb 42

Authentic Low Carb Dips 42

Tomatillo Salsa..42

Pico De Gallo 45

Bean Dip 47

Guacamole..49

Corn Salsa 51

7 Layer Dip 53

Basic Salsa 55

Tirokafteri..57

Layered Mediterranean...59

Queso 61

Chapter Four: Dessert Style Dips Made Low Carb 63

Dessert Dips Turned Low Carb...63

Walnut Chocolate Fruit Dip...63

Peanut Butter Cheesecake Dip 66

Cheesecake Dip 68

Strawberry Fruit Dip 69

Peanut Butter Cup Dip 71

Low Carb Cookie Dough Dip 72

Honey Ricotta Dip 74

Fruit Dip 75

Pumpkin Dip 77

Berry Good Dip 78

Chapter Five: Other Fun and Healthy Dips 80

Fun and Healthy Dips for Every Occasion 80

Taco Dip 80

Smoked Fish Dip 83

French Onion Dip 85

Pizza Dip 86

Clam Dip 88

Cream Cheese Dip 90

Crab Dip 91

Chili Dip 93

BLT Dip 94

Caramelized Sweet Onion Dip 96

Best Practices & Common Mistakes 98

Do's 98

Don'ts 99

Conclusion 101

Author's Foreword

"You gain strength, courage, and confidence by every experience in which you really stop to look fear in the face...You must do the thing you think you cannot do." – Eleanor Roosevelt

One of the biggest struggles I have faced in adopting a healthy lifestyle is attending or hosting parties. It seems temptation is around every corner when you attend a party thrown by friends or co-workers. Every table you can see is covered with high calorie, carb loaded, fatty dips and appetizers. It is so easy to tell yourself I will just have one bite or just one night won't hurt my goal. The truth is you can never have just one bite and even detouring from your new lifestyle plan for just one night can have disastrous results.

I knew I needed to find a solution and fast as the holiday season was soon approaching. We all know how hard it can be to resist temptation during the year, but the holiday season is filled with nothing but parties and bad food choices calling our names. Denying yourself the ability to indulge in the holiday parties often makes the carvings worse, which can cause further setbacks. The solution is to find dips that are geared towards your new healthy lifestyle.

Everybody probably has horror stories about horrible tasting foods, especially when they are making a switch in their diet. The key to sticking to a healthy lifestyle is to find recipes that fit your new lifestyle, but still taste good. It was my intention to go out and find those kinds of recipes, so I could enjoy the holiday season without having to give up my healthy lifestyle. I am happy to say that I have been able to accomplish that and now I can't wait to share what I have found with you.

Bonus: Your FREE Gift

As a token of our appreciation, please take advantage of the **FREE Gift** - a lifetime **VIP Membership** at our book club.

Follow the link below to download your FREE books:

http://bit.ly/vipbookclub

As a VIP member, you will get an instant **FREE** access to exclusive new releases and bestselling books.

Chapter One: Creating Healthy and Fun Dips For Parties

"And make me do my sits when I finish my dips" – Harlem World

In this chapter, I will help you to:

- Choose the right dip to make

- Make the perfect party dip

Picking the Dip

If you have ever been to a party, you should already know just how important dips are. Whether it is a holiday office party, a backyard BBQ, or just an informal get together at your house, dips are usually the center attraction. Food spreads are often set out before the guests start arriving and the one thing that everybody goes for first, no matter what appetizers are on the table, is the various dips that are on display. Making the perfect dip and choosing the right dippers for your dip are the best way to make a great first impression, which means making your dip the hit of the party.

The first thing you need to think about when making the perfect party dip is what kind of dip you are going to make. Choosing the right dip for the occasion is vital to ensuring your dip is the first one to disappear off of the table rather than the first one to end up in the garbage when the party is over.

The first thing to consider is the occasion, is it an informal or formal one. Informal parties give you more options when it comes to picking the perfect dip, such as the traditional Lipton Onion Dip. A formal party requires dips that are more like a spread than a traditional dip. Always match your dip to the occasion on hand.

Seasons also play a role in deciding on the perfect party dip. The best example of his is summer parties are often outdoors where the weather is hot. The last thing anybody wants at a summer party on a hot day is a hot dip. Summer parties call for cool and creamy dips, while hot dips are best served during the cooler months when parties are kept indoors.

The other thing you need to keep in mind when picking the perfect party dip is what is being served at the party. Some party dips pair well with certain dishes. For example, vegetable and fruit dips are ideal choices for backyard BBQs. Crab, fish, and clam dips go great with crackers and can be served with soups or other hot entrees. Salsa and guacamole go great with Mexican inspired dishes.

However, the most important thing to keep in mind when deciding what party dip or dips to make for your next get-together is what you are in the mood for. It is always more fun to make things that you are in the mood to eat. Plus if you make something you are in the mood for, you are going to enjoy the party even more.

Making the Perfect Party Dip

Now that you have decided what dip would go perfectly with the party you are planning or attending, the next step is to make the dip. Many people assume that dips are simply made by throwing a bunch of ingredients together and mixing them up. While his general idea might be true, there is a lot more that goes into making the perfect dip.

In order to make and present the perfect party dip I have assembled some easy to follow dips to ensure that your dip always turns out just right.

- How you mix your dip is going to affect the overall taste of your dip. If you are after a creamy and smooth dip you are going to want to whip it together until you reach the desired consistency. If you are making more of a sauce like a dip you are going to want to beat it until you have achieved your desired results.

- If your dip calls for cream cheese I have learned that softening beforehand allows for creamy results. Trying to beat cold cream cheese leaves the dip lumpy. To soften the cream cheese simply leave it out on the counter for a couple of hours before using. You can also soften it in the microwave, but be careful of overheating it.

- If your dip is a hot dip you want to make sure that you are not cooking it or storing it at too high of a temperature. If the dip is too hot when people try to eat it, the dip is going to alter the taste of the snacks. Dips need to be the right temperature based on the dippers you are serving them with.

- How your dip appears to others is very important. You want a dip that is going to grab people's attention; it increases the chance of them wanting to try it. The best way to grab people's attention is to use striking colors, something that will really stand out. White dips are often paired great with colorful vegetables, think of a vegetable tray. Colorful dips can be used with bread and crackers, as long as it will create the desired taste.

- Your dips are made to enhance the flavor of the dippers that you choose. When making a dip ensure that you are choosing a dipper whose flavor will be enhanced rather than dulled or overpowered by the dip.

- If you are making dip for a large number of people you want to choose recipe that is easy to double or even triple. Or you can simply pick a dip whose original recipe makes enough to feed a large crowd.

- When making dips that contain guacamole you want to prevent the guacamole from turning brown. The best way to do that is to press plastic wrap directly onto the guacamole's surface.

- Cold dips need to be kept cold even during transport. Transporting them in an insulated cooler with ice packs is the ideal way to safely transport them and keep them at temperature. Warm dips can also be safely transported in insulated containers, but without ice.

- Some dips can be frozen for up to one week to help preserve their freshness, but sometimes freezing the dips will alter their texture. You can help correct the texture by whisking the dip upon thawing; adding fresh diary to the dip, or you can even try reheating the dip. The best dips to freeze are the ones that contain hard cheeses. Dips with high water content should not be frozen.

- Transporting dips can alter their appearance. If transporting a layered dip, do so in a container that has an extremely tight lid. The tighter the lid the less chance of the layers moving around. Creamy dips can be transported in Ziploc bags and then transferred to a serving dish or platter upon arrival. This is recommended for dips that will be using foods as their serving platter.

- When keeping hot dips warm be careful of your heat setting. If it's too warm the edges of the dip will become crusty and the bottom of the dip can actually burn. Stirring the dip even when it is sitting will help prevent this from happening.

- Some dips require mashing, such as guacamole. The key to making these kinds of dips is to make sure you don't mash them too much. You want to do a rough mash versus a fine mash to ensure the right consistency is reached. You want chunks of avocados in your guacamole.

- Always taste your dips as you are making them. Sure recipes call for a certain amount of spices, but you can always later your dips to meet your tastes. You might find as you make the dip that you need more or less of the various spices that the dip calls for. Use the recipes as a guideline, not as an absolute.

What are the Best Dippers for Dips?

Pairing your dip with the right dippers is also vital to the success of your dip. As I mentioned earlier your dip is supposed to enhance the flavor of the dipper, it is meant to compliment the item you are dipping. The dip is not meant to overpower the dipper. The biggest challenge I faced when making the switch to a healthier lifestyle was finding healthy dippers to use for a variety of dips. I spent a lot of time researching various dippers and their nutritional content, so I want to take a moment to share some of my finds with you.

Vegetables

Out of all of the dippers available to use this option is by far the healthiest option. Not to mention vegetables also provide the most color, think about those super colorful vegetable trays. The best part about using vegetables as a dipper is you can use them with a large variety of dips. Cool and creamy dips, such as dill dips, are great for all vegetables. You can even pair vegetables with spinach, onion, and hummus dips. Just pick the right tasting vegetable for the dip at hand.

Chips

Many dips, such as onion and guacamole, simply do not taste right unless they are on a chip of some sort. The problem with chips is they are greasy, plus they are not exactly considered to be low carb. One way to solve this problem is to make your own chips with corn tortillas rather than flour tortillas. Corn chips can easily be made with corn tortillas, simply cut them into triangles, brush with olive oil and sprinkle with some salt and bake them until crispy. Pork rinds are another good substitution for chips.

Breads/Crackers

The majority of the dips listed in this book are great paired with breads or served on crackers. To follow my healthier lifestyle choices I simply use my low carb breads and crackers for my dips. You can make your own low carb products or you can purchase them in stores. One of my favorite things to dip in some of the dessert style dips is cinnamon crisps, which I make with low carb flat breads brushed with melted butter, sprinkled with cinnamon sugar and then baked for about 8 minutes at 350 degrees.

Fruits

If you are looking for low carb this is an area where you need to be really careful. Not all fruits are good choices for a low carb lifestyle. If you do wish to dip fruit in some of the sweeter dips you can opt for berries, watermelon, cantaloupe, honeydew, and peaches. Most other fruits have a higher carb count, so they should be eaten on rare occasions.

Meat

This might seem a little odd to those of you who are new to low carb diets, but this is an excellent choice to use for dipping. Meat on a stick is an excellent choice for cheese based dips, such as queso. Some meats to use include sausage or beef that has been grilled or even meatballs.

Chapter Two: Vegan and Vegetarian-Friendly Dips

"People eat meat and think they will become strong as an ox, forgetting that the ox eats grass." – Pino Caruso

In this chapter, I'll help you to:

- Vegan dips for parties
- Vegetarian dips everyone will enjoy

Best Vegan Dips for Parties

You may have multiple sections...

Baba Ghanoush Dip/Spread

Prep Time	15 mins.
Cook Time	45 mins.
Serving Size	10 servings
Calories	115
Carbs	11 g
Fat	8 g
Protein	3 g

Ingredients

- 3 lbs. eggplant
- 3 tbsp. olive oil
- 1/3 c. tahini
- 2 garlic gloves
- ½ c. lemon juice
- Salt and pepper

Let's Cook:

1. Rub outside of eggplants with olive oil and place in roasting pan. Roast at 450 degrees for 20 minutes. Skins will be charred and inside will be tender.

2. Remove seeds and peel eggplant once it has cooled. Chop up the insides and place in a food processor.

3. Add tahini, crushed garlic, salt, pepper, and lemon juice. Mix on low speed until coarse paste forms. You can add a few tablespoons of water to help thin out the mixture some.

Tzatziki

Prep Time	15 mins.
Cook Time	2 hours
Serving Size	4 servings
Calories	128.4
Carbs	6.1 g
Fat	9.2 g
Protein	6.5 g

Ingredients

- 12 oz. box of silken tofu
- 3 tbsp. lemon juice
- 1 tbsp. white wine vinegar
- 2 garlic cloves
- ½ tsp. salt
- 2 tbsp. olive oil
- 1 cucumber, remove seeds and grate

Let's Cook:

1. Add tofu, salt, vinegar and lemon juice to a blender and mix until smooth.

2. Add chopped garlic and oil and mix some more. Pour mixture into a serving bowl.

3. Squeeze excess water out of cucumber with hands and add to dip.

4. Stir gently, add any fresh herbs, and stir again.

5. Place in fridge and chill for 2 hours before serving.

Extra Tip:

One of the great things about this amazing dip is you can add fresh dill or fresh mint. What one you add will depend on your unique tastes or what you are serving the dip with. On average you can add about a tablespoon of fresh dill or mint, but like all seasonings you can use more or less depending on your taste.

Artichoke Hearts

Prep Time	10 mins.
Cook Time	20 mins.
Serving Size	6 servings
Calories	151.9
Carbs	16.6 g
Fat	5.5 g
Protein	13.8 g

Ingredients

- ½ yellow onion
- 8 oz. marinated artichoke hearts
- 12 oz. frozen chopped spinach
- 1 tbsp. olive oil
- 12 oz. silken tofu, firm
- 2 tbsp. apple cider vinegar
- 3 garlic cloves
- ½ c. nutritional yeast
- 1 tsp. dried basil

- 1 tsp. dried parsley

- ¼ tsp. cayenne pepper

- 1 tsp. salt

- ½ tsp. pepper

Let's Cook:

1. Over medium high heat sauté artichoke hearts, onion, and spinach for 6 minutes, you want the onion to be soft.

2. Place yeast, tofu, garlic, vinegar, and various spices into a blender and mix until smooth.

3. Pour blender mixture into a bowl and mix in spinach mixture. Mix well.

4. Pour mixture into a non-stick baking dish and bake at 350 degrees for 20 minutes. The top should be lightly browned.

Extra Tip:

Although this recipe calls for the use of dried herbs you can easily substitute fresh herbs. If you wish to substitute you will need to use three times more of the fresh herbs than the dried herbs called for in this recipe. Dried herbs are quite a bit more potent than fresh, so you have to adjust accordingly to achieve the same wonderful taste.

Onion Dip

Prep Time	15 mins.
Cook Time	0 mins.
Serving Size	8 servings
Calories	249.1
Carbs	6.6 g
Fat	25.4 g
Protein	2.9 g

Ingredients

- 2 c. macadamia nuts
- ¾ c. water
- 1 tsp. sea salt
- 1 garlic clove
- 1 c. onion

Let's Cook:

1. Soak macadamia nuts in water for several hours to help soften them.

2. Drain the water from the macadamia nuts, place nuts. Water, sea salt, and garlic into a blender and blend until smooth.

3. Pour into a bowl, fold in onions and mix gently. Place in fridge to chill.

Carrot Hummus

Prep Time	15 mins.
Cook Time	0 mins.
Serving Size	6 servings
Calories	177.8
Carbs	23.6 g
Fat	7.8 g
Protein	5.1 g

Ingredients

- 1 c. grated carrots
- 1 c. chickpeas, cooked
- 2 tbsp. lemon juice
- 2 tbsp. tahini
- 2 green onions
- 1 tbsp. olive oil

Let's Cook:

1. Add chickpeas, lemon juice, onions, olive oil, and tahini to a food processor. Mix until you have a

smooth paste. Add a small amount of water if you are having problems with the consistency.

2. Gently mix in the grated carrots and serve.

Vegetarian Dips Everyone Will Love

Red Bell Pepper Dip

Prep Time	10 mins.
Cook Time	2 mins.
Serving Size	8 servings
Calories	6.6
Carbs	1.5 g
Fat	0 g
Protein	0.3 g

Ingredients

- 7 oz. jar roasted red peppers
- ½ c. Fat-free cream cheese
- 2 scallions
- 1 garlic clove
- 1 tbsp. lemon juice

Let's Cook:

1. Add all ingredients into a blender and process until thoroughly pureed.

2. Pour into a bowl and chill for a few hours before serving.

4. Direction 2

Dill Dip

Prep Time	10 mins.
Cook Time	0 mins.
Serving Size	8 servings
Calories	162.8
Carbs	7.2 g
Fat	14.6 g
Protein	1.6 g

Ingredients

- 1 c. sour cream
- ½ c. mayonnaise
- 1 tbsp. dill weed
- 1 tbsp. parsley flakes
- 1 tbsp. minced onion
- ½ tsp. celery seed
- 1/8 tsp. garlic powder
- ¼ tsp. seasoning salt

Let's Cook:

1. Place all ingredients into a medium sized mixing bowl and stir well.

2. Place dip in the fridge for several hours to chill before serving.

Cheese and Herb Dip

Prep Time	5 mins.
Cook Time	0 mins.
Serving Size	8 servings
Calories	87
Carbs	1.5 g
Fat	7.9 g
Protein	2.8 g

Ingredients

- ½ c. sour cream
- ¼ c. cream cheese
- ¼ c. goat cheese
- 2 tbsp. chives
- 1 tbsp. parsley
- 1 tbsp. tarragon
- 1 garlic clove

Let's Cook:

1. Place all ingredients into a blender and blend until smooth.

2. Taste and season with salt and pepper, if desired.

3. Pour into serving bowl, cover, and chill for a couple of hours before serving.

Extra Tip:

All of the herbs used in this party dip are supposed to be fresh. You can use dried herbs if that is all you have on hand, but will need to make some adjustments to the amount of herbs called for. Dried herbs are three times more potent than fresh herbs, so with dried less is always better. If you want a little spice to this dip, add a single red chili pepper that has been deseeded and finely chopped.

Edamame Dip

Prep Time	10 mins.
Cook Time	0 mins.
Serving Size	8 servings
Calories	166.4
Carbs	20 g
Fat	5.2 g
Protein	11.8 g

Ingredients

- 1 ½ c. shelled edamame, cooked
- ½ c. water
- ¼ c. red onion
- 3 tbsp. fresh cilantro
- 2 tbsp. rice vinegar
- 1 tbsp. olive oil
- ½ tsp. salt
- 16 oz. white beans, drained
- 1 ½ chili garlic sauce

Let's Cook:

1. If edamame is frozen, thaw it out and then cook it before shelling it. Drain the can of white beans and set aside.

2. Add all ingredients to a food processor. Blend on low until smooth.

3. Pour dip into serving bowl, cover and refrigerate for a couple of hours before serving.

Roasted Pumpkin Dip

Prep Time	5 mins.
Cook Time	30 mins.
Serving Size	1 bowl
Calories	198.5
Carbs	8.6 g
Fat	16.3 g
Protein	8.1 g

Ingredients

- 1 butternut pumpkin
- 1 tsp. ground cumin
- 2 tbsp. peanut butter, crunchy
- ¼ oz. chili sauce
- Olive oil

Let's Cook:

1. Roast the pumpkin in a 350-degree oven until soft and tender, about 30 minutes.
2. Scoop out flesh from inside of the pumpkin and mash it.

3. Add ground cumin, peanut butter, and chili sauce to mashed pumpkin and stir to mix well.

4. Drizzle in some olive and stir again.

Chapter Three: Authentic Inspired Dips Turned Low Carb

> *"Junk speech is as bad for you as junk food. Use healthy words to describe your body." – Bexlife.com*

In this chapter, I'll help you to:

- Authentic low carb dips
- Low carb dips

Authentic Low Carb Dips

Tomatillo Salsa

Prep Time	40 mins.
Cook Time	40 mins.
Serving Size	1 pint
Calories	89.1
Carbs	18.6 g
Fat	1.7 g
Protein	2.7 g

Ingredients

- 6 c. chopped tomatillos
- 3 c. chopped onions
- 3 jalapeno peppers
- 6 garlic cloves
- ½ c. cilantro
- ½ c. lemon juice
- 2 tsp. cumin
- 1 tbsp. salt
- 1 tsp. pepper

Let's Cook:

1. Chop the peppers, onions, garlic, cilantro, and tomatillos. Once chopped place everything into a large pot over high heat. Stir frequently until boiling.
2. Reduce heat and simmer for 20 minutes.

3. Can ladle into pint sized jars and process in a hot water bath to store for future use or you can store in the refrigerator for immediate use.

Pico De Gallo

Prep Time	20 mins.
Cook Time	0 mins.
Serving Size	1 ½ cups
Calories	25.3
Carbs	5.7 g
Fat	0.2 g
Protein	1.1 g

Ingredients

- 3 large tomatoes
- ½ c. onion
- 2 garlic cloves
- 2 jalapeno peppers
- 3 tbsp. cilantro
- 1 tbsp. olive oil
- 1 tbsp. lime juice

Let's Cook:

1. Core tomatoes and remove seeds. Remove seeds from jalapeno peppers.

2. Finely chop tomatoes, onions, and cilantro. Mince garlic and jalapenos.

3. Mix all ingredients together in a mixing bowl and allow to sit for 15 minutes.

Bean Dip

Prep Time	10 mins.
Cook Time	10 mins.
Serving Size	1 ¼ cup
Calories	134.6
Carbs	12.3 g
Fat	6 g
Protein	11.1 g

Ingredients

- 1 ½ c. shelled edamame
- 1/3 c. salsa
- 1 green onion
- 2 tbsp. fresh cilantro, leaves only
- ¼ tsp. Mexican seasoning (can make own or use store bought)

Let's Cook:

1. Cook and shell frozen edamame.
2. Place all ingredients into a food processor and blend until smooth.

Extra Tip:

You can make your own Mexican seasoning by mixing together 1/8 tsp. cayenne pepper, 1/8 tsp. black pepper, 4 tsp. ground cumin, ¼ tsp. garlic powder, and 5 tsp. chili powder.

Guacamole

Prep Time	10 mins.
Cook Time	0 mins.
Serving Size	6 servings
Calories	45.6
Carbs	3.8 g
Fat	3.6 g
Protein	0.8 g

Ingredients

- 1 large avocado
- 2 plum tomatoes
- ½ onion
- ¼ c. cilantro
- 1 jalapeno pepper
- 1 tbsp. lime juice
- ½ tsp. salt
- ¼ tsp. pepper

Let's Cook:

1. Cut avocado in half and remove the pit. Scrape pulp from each half and place into a small bowl.

2. Use a potato masher or fork and coarsely mash the pulp together. Add remaining ingredients and stir gently until just combined.

Corn Salsa

Prep Time	10 mins.
Cook Time	0 mins.
Serving Size	4 cups
Calories	131
Carbs	28 g
Fat	2.3 g
Protein	4.2 g

Ingredients

- 15 oz. whole kernel corn
- ½ c. green pepper
- ½ c. red bell pepper
- ½ c. red onion
- 2 tomatoes
- ¼ c. black olives
- 2 tbsp. pickled jalapeno peppers
- 1 tsp. pickled jalapeno pepper juice
- 2 tbsp. red wine vinegar

- ½ tsp. garlic salt

- ½ tsp. pepper

Let's Cook:

1. Chop up all of the vegetables. Drain and rinse the corn.

2. Place all ingredients inside of a mixing bowl and mix well.

3. Cover and place in the fridge for several hours to chill.

7 Layer Dip

Prep Time	10 mins.
Cook Time	0 mins.
Serving Size	½ cup
Calories	138.5
Carbs	11.1 g
Fat	8.7 g
Protein	5.4 g

Ingredients

- 16 oz. refried beans
- Taco Seasoning/Mexican Seasoning
- 1 c. sour cream
- 1 c. guacamole
- 1 c. salsa
- 1 c. lettuce
- 1 c. cheese
- 4 oz. sliced olives
- 1 c. tomatoes

Let's Cook:

1. Assemble all of your ingredients and find a baking dish that will allow you to create seven separate layers.

2. Mix together beans with Mexican seasoning or taco seasoning.

3. Layer the dip in this order: beans, sour cream, guacamole, salsa, lettuce, cheese, olives, and tomatoes.

Extra Tip:

One of the great things about this dip is the ingredients. You can use all store bought products or you can make your own guacamole, salsa, and seasoning from recipes found in this book. You can even leave out specific layers if you wish.

Basic Salsa

Prep Time	45 mins.
Cook Time	30 mins.
Serving Size	1/8 cup
Calories	12.5
Carbs	2.9 g
Fat	0.1 g
Protein	0.4 g

Ingredients

- 8 c. tomatoes
- 2 ½ c. onions
- 1 ½ c. green peppers
- 1 c. jalapeno pepper
- 6 garlic cloves
- 2 tsp. cumin
- 2 tsp. pepper
- 1/3 c. vinegar
- 1/3 c. granulated sweetener

- 15 oz. tomato sauce

- 12 oz. tomato paste

- 1/8 c. canning salt

Let's Cook:

1. Wash, peel, and remove seeds of the various ingredients. Chop all vegetables and place in a pot.

2. Add spices and other remaining ingredients and cook over medium heat until boiling. Lower heat and boil slowly for about 10 minutes.

3. Pour into jars and seal canning jars. Continue cooking in a hot water bath for 10 minutes.

Extra Tip:

This is a chunky salsa, so how rough or fine you chop your vegetables will determine how chunky your salsa will be. Rough chopped means bigger chunks in the salsa, while finely chopped is more liquid. You can, can all of it for later use or you can leave some in the refrigerator for immediate use.

Tirokafteri

Prep Time	15 mins.
Cook Time	70 mins.
Serving Size	¼ cup
Calories	181.9
Carbs	2.5 g
Fat	16.1 g
Protein	7.2 g

Ingredients

- 2 c. feta cheese
- 1 hot pepper
- 1 tbsp. vinegar
- 4 tbsp. olive oil
- ½ tsp. oregano

Let's Cook:

1. Place feta cheese in a small bowl, add some water and allow to sit for one hour. Drain and cut cheese into cubes.

2. Grill pepper, cut open and remove seeds, and then chop the pepper into pieces.

3. Place cheese cubes into a mixing bowl along with the pepper pieces. Use an electric mixer to beat the cheese and peppers together.

4. Add vinegar and slowly add olive oil while you are mixing.

5. Stir in oregano and serve.

Layered Mediterranean

Prep Time	10 mins.
Cook Time	0 mins.
Serving Size	¼ cup
Calories	93.4
Carbs	2.6 g
Fat	7.9 g
Protein	3.8 g

Ingredients

- 8 oz. fat-free cream cheese
- 1 ¼ c. feta cheese
- 2 tbsp. milk of choice
- 1 tbsp. dried basil
- 10 oz. frozen spinach
- 1 tomato
- 3 green onions
- ¼ c. sliced black olives

Let's Cook:

1. Allow the cream cheese to soften, crumble the feta cheese, and thaw and drain spinach.

2. Beat together softened cream cheese, 1 cup feta cheese, milk, and basil until well blended.

3. Spread mixture out on the bottom of a 9-inch pie pan.

4. Spread spinach, chopped tomato, green onions, and sliced olives on the top and sprinkle with remaining feta cheese.

5. Cover and refrigerate for 1 hour before serving.

Queso

Prep Time	5 mins.
Cook Time	15 mins.
Serving Size	4 servings
Calories	126.9
Carbs	17.8 g
Fat	4.6 g
Protein	6.2 g

Ingredients

- ¼ c. flour, unbleached
- ¼ c. nutritional yeast
- 1 tsp. salt
- 1 tsp. paprika
- ½ tsp. garlic powder
- 2 tbsp. fat-free margarine
- 1 c. salsa
- 1 c. water

Let's Cook:

1. Place all dry ingredients into a small saucepan and then add the water.

2. Over medium heat whisk the mixture constantly until thoroughly combined.

3. Add margarine and salsa and continue whisking for two more minutes.

Extra Tip:

With this recipe you must whisk the entire time you are cooking. If you do not constantly whisk the mixture the flour will become lumpy. The lumps will be lumps of flour, which will alter the taste of the otherwise smooth and creamy dip.

Chapter Four: Dessert Style Dips Made Low Carb

"If you are persistent, you will get it. If you are consistent, you will keep it." – Meredith Schneider

In this chapter, I will help you to:

- Sweet party dips
- Amazing dessert dips

Dessert Dips Turned Low Carb

Walnut Chocolate Fruit Dip

Prep Time	10 mins.
Cook Time	0 mins.
Serving Size	20 servings
Calories	58.8
Carbs	2.7 g
Fat	5.2 g
Protein	1 g

Ingredients

- 1 c. walnuts
- 6 dates
- 2 tbsp. cocoa
- 2 tbsp. agave nectar
- 1 tsp. vanilla extract
- 2 tbsp. olive oil
- 3 tbsp. water

Let's Cook:

1. Soak dates in some water for several hours to help soften them up.
2. Finely chop walnuts in a food processor, you want a fine ground.
3. Add dates to the walnuts one at a time. Grind each date until you can no longer tell it is in there.
4. Add sweetener, cocoa, and vanilla and continue to process on low.

5. Slowly add a small amount of oil and then water. Alternate between the two until you have reached the desired consistency.

Peanut Butter Cheesecake Dip

Prep Time	5 mins.
Cook Time	0 mins.
Serving Size	2 tbsp.
Calories	164
Carbs	2.3 g
Fat	16.6 g
Protein	3.5 g

Ingredients

- 8 oz. softened cream cheese
- ½ unsweetened peanut butter
- ½ c. butter
- 1 tsp. vanilla extract
- ¼ tsp. salt
- 1 tsp. vanilla liquid stevia

Let's Cook:

1. Allow butter and cream cheese to come to room temperature.

2. Place all ingredients into a bowl or stand mixer. Mix together until thoroughly combined. The mixture should be smooth.

3. Can taste and adjust sweetener.

Cheesecake Dip

Prep Time	5 mins.
Cook Time	0 mins.
Serving Size	2 tbsp.
Calories	195
Carbs	3 g
Fat	18.3 g
Protein	7.9 g

Ingredients

- 1 c. sour cream
- ½ c. cream cheese
- ¼ c. vanilla whey protein
- 2 tsp. Sugar-free vanilla extract
- 2 tbsp. Swerve

Let's Cook:

1. Place all ingredients into a mixing bowl and mix until thoroughly combined.

Strawberry Fruit Dip

Prep Time	10 mins.
Cook Time	60 mins.
Serving Size	1/3 cup
Calories	157.9
Carbs	7.4 g
Fat	14.1 g
Protein	1.3 g

Ingredients

- 1 c. sliced strawberries
- ¼ c. sour cream
- 1 tbsp. granulated sweetener
- ¼ tsp. vanilla
- ½ c. whipping cream

Let's Cook:

1. Blend together strawberries, sugar, vanilla, and sour cream in a blender until smooth.
2. In a small bowl beat the cream until peaks form.

3. Fold whipped cream into strawberry mixture.

4. Cover and place in refrigerator for 1 hour.

Peanut Butter Cup Dip

Prep Time	5 mins.
Cook Time	0 mins.
Serving Size	2 tbsp.
Calories	164
Carbs	2.3 g
Fat	14.6 g
Protein	3.5 g

Ingredients

- 8 oz. cream cheese, softened

- ½ c. peanut butter, sugar-free

- ¼ c. Stevia

- ¼ c. Dark Mini Chocolate Chips

Let's Cook:

1. Place all ingredients into a mixing bowl and mix until thoroughly combined. The mixture will be a smooth consistency.

Low Carb Cookie Dough Dip

Prep Time	5 mins.
Cook Time	0 mins.
Serving Size	1 of 2
Calories	170
Carbs	11 g
Fat	2 g
Protein	25 g

Ingredients

- 8 oz, yogurt choice
- 1 scoop protein powder
- 1 tbsp. granulated sweetener
- 1 tbsp. coconut flour
- Chocolate chips

Let's Cook:

1. In a mixing bowl mix together yogurt, sweetener, and protein powder until well combined.

2. Add coconut flour a little at a time and continue stirring. Only add enough coconut flour to reach your desired consistency.

3. Sprinkle chocolate chips on top and serve.

Extra Tip:

If you want a thick dip you will need to use a full 2 tablespoons of coconut flour. If you prefer a thinner dip use one tablespoon and some milk of your choice until you reach the desired consistency. This recipe is perfect for one person, will need to double or triple it if making for a crowd.

Honey Ricotta Dip

Prep Time	2 mins.
Cook Time	0 mins.
Serving Size	¼ cup
Calories	123
Carbs	5 g
Fat	8.1 g
Protein	7.1 g

Ingredients

- 1 c. ricotta cheese
- 1 tbsp. milk of choice
- 2 tsp. honey
- 1 tsp. vanilla extract

Let's Cook:

1. Combine all ingredients together in a mixing bowl and beat together until well combined.

Fruit Dip

Prep Time	2 mins.
Cook Time	0 mins.
Serving Size	1/8 cup
Calories	99.9
Carbs	1.7 g
Fat	10 g
Protein	1.2 g

Ingredients

- 10 oz. heavy cream
- 1 c. yogurt

Let's Cook:

1. Using a handheld mixer, whip the heavy cream until thickened.
2. Add in the yogurt and stir to mix well.
3. Chill in refrigerate until ready to serve.

Extra Tip:

With this recipe you can use any kind of yogurt you want. Greek yogurt is my go-to choice, but I have also used light yogurts. You can use any flavor, the flavor you choose will affect the flavor. One of my favorite yogurts to use is vanilla, but strawberry is also a nice taste.

Pumpkin Dip

Prep Time	5 mins.
Cook Time	0 mins.
Serving Size	1/8 cup
Calories	34.9
Carbs	2.3 g
Fat	2.3 g
Protein	1.3 g

Ingredients

- 8 oz. fat-free cream cheese
- ½ c. canned pumpkin
- 2 tbsp. taco seasoning mix
- 1/8 tsp. garlic powder
- ½ c. chopped bell pepper

Let's Cook:

1. Using a hand mixer beat together the first four ingredients in the list until smooth.
2. Mix in the bell pepper and chill until ready to serve.

Berry Good Dip

Prep Time	15 mins.
Cook Time	0 mins.
Serving Size	¼ cup
Calories	104.6
Carbs	6.6 g
Fat	8.4 g
Protein	1.5 g

Ingredients

- 8 oz. frozen strawberries
- 4 oz. softened fat-free cream cheese
- ¼ c. Fat-free sour cream
- 1 tbsp. granulated sweetener

Let's Cook:

1. Add strawberries to a blender and process until smooth.
2. In a small bowl beat cream cheese with a handheld mixture until smooth.

3. Mix in sour cream, strawberry, and sugar; stir until thoroughly combined.

4. Place in refrigerator until ready to serve.

Extra Tip:

This recipe calls for frozen strawberries and fat-free cream cheese, but you can make different adjustments based on your own tastes. Since the strawberries have to be thawed out before using, you can use fresh strawberries, but must remove stems first. Fat-free cream cheese can be switched with regular cream cheese for a sweeter taste.

Chapter Five: Other Fun and Healthy Dips

"You may never know what results come of your actions, but if you do nothing, there will be no results." – Mahatma Gandhi

In this chapter, I will help you to:

- Fun party dips

- Healthy chip dips

Fun and Healthy Dips for Every Occasion

Taco Dip

Prep Time	20 mins.
Cook Time	0 mins.
Serving Size	1/3 cup
Calories	128.9
Carbs	5.5 g
Fat	8 g
Protein	5.3 g

Ingredients

- 16 oz. refried beans
- 8 oz. fat-free sour cream
- 3 avocados
- 16 oz. shredded cheese
- 10 oz. taco sauce
- ½ c. chopped black olives
- ½ c. chopped scallions
- 1 ½ c. chopped tomatoes
- 1 small onion, chopped
- 1 tsp. chili powder
- 1 tsp. garlic powder
- 1 tsp. pepper

Let's Cook:

1. Spread beans along the bottom of a casserole dish. You can even use a pie pan.

2. Cut and pit avocados, remove flesh and mash together with chili powder, onion, pepper, and garlic. Layer avocado mixture over beans.

3. Spread sour cream over the avocado mixture.

4. Mix together cheese, taco sauce, olives, scallions, and tomatoes. Pour over sour cream.

Extra Tip:

This taco dip can be made as mild or as hot as you would like. You can use different strength taco sauce, such as hot or mild. You can also add a small amount of jalapeno sauce if you want to give your dip some extra kick.

Smoked Fish Dip

Prep Time	5 mins.
Cook Time	0 mins.
Serving Size	1/3 cup
Calories	216
Carbs	3.4 g
Fat	14.1 g
Protein	19.3 g

Ingredients

- ¾ lb. smoked white fish fillet
- 8 oz. softened fat-free cream cheese
- 3 tbsp. cream
- 2 tbsp. lemon juice
- ¼ tsp. garlic salt
- 1 tsp. grated onion

Let's Cook:

1. Allow cream cheese to soften at room temperature.

2. Flake white fish into a food processor, double checking for bones.

3. Add remaining ingredients and pulse until smooth.

4. Place in refrigerator for several hours before serving to allow flavors to mesh.

French Onion Dip

Prep Time	5 mins.
Cook Time	0 mins.
Serving Size	1/8 cup
Calories	82.1
Carbs	2.9 g
Fat	3.4 g
Protein	1.4 g

Ingredients

- 6 tbsp. Fat-free sour cream
- 2 tsp. minced onion
- 2 tsp. beef bouillon granules

Let's Cook:

1. In a small bowl mix together all ingredients until thoroughly combined.
2. Place in refrigerator for at least 30 minutes prior to serving.

Pizza Dip

Prep Time	15 mins.
Cook Time	20 mins.
Serving Size	¼ cup
Calories	172.1
Carbs	2.8 g
Fat	10.8 g
Protein	5.1 g

Ingredients

- 8 oz. fat-free cream cheese
- 1 tsp. oregano
- ½ c. pepperoni slices
- ¼ c. chopped green onion
- ½ c. Fat-free sour cream
- ½ c. pizza sauce
- ¼ c. chopped bell pepper
- ¼ c. grated mozzarella cheese

Let's Cook:

1. Mix all ingredients, except cheese, together in a large mixing bowl.

2. Pour into a baking dish and bake for 15 minutes at 350 degrees.

3. Remove from oven top with cheese and bake for an additional 5 minutes or until cheese is melted.

Extra Tip:

One of the great things about this recipe is you can easily adjust it to your own tastes. You can leave out the pepperoni, which lowers the overall fat content. You can always add in your favorite pizza toppings, such as black olives or pineapple. You can also add the cheese in at the beginning and simply top with more cheese. Onions can also be used as a garnish.

Clam Dip

Prep Time	6 mins.
Cook Time	0 mins.
Serving Size	¼ cup
Calories	183.5
Carbs	5.2 g
Fat	10.5 g
Protein	10.4 g

Ingredients

- 1 minced garlic clove
- 8 oz. fat-free cream cheese
- 2 tsp. lemon juice
- 1 ½ tsp. Worcestershire sauce
- ½ tsp. salt
- 7 oz. canned clams
- ¼ c. clam juice

Let's Cook:

1. Drain the clams, but reserve the juice to use as the clam juice.

2. Place all ingredients into a bowl and blend until smooth.

Cream Cheese Dip

Prep Time	15 mins.
Cook Time	0 mins.
Serving Size	1/8 cup
Calories	40.4
Carbs	1.1 g
Fat	3.8 g
Protein	0.8 g

Ingredients

- 8 oz. fat-free cream cheese
- 3 tbsp. Mayonnaise
- 1 tsp. garlic powder
- 1/3 red pepper
- 1/3 green pepper
- 3 slices of red onion

Let's Cook:

1. Finely dice peppers and onion.

2. In a small bowl mix together cream cheese, mayonnaise, and garlic powder. Can add more garlic based on taste preferences.

3. Stir in vegetables and mix well.

4. Refrigerate for one hour to allow flavors to mix.

5. Pull out several minutes before serving to allow dip to soften.

Crab Dip

Prep Time	10 mins.
Cook Time	10 mins.
Serving Size	½ cup
Calories	189.4
Carbs	2.6 g
Fat	13.4 g
Protein	14.4 g

Ingredients

- 1/8 tsp. Worcestershire sauce
- Dash of Tabasco
- 14 oz. crab meat

- 2 tbsp. horseradish
- 8 oz. fat-free cream cheese
- ¼ of an onion, minced

Let's Cook:

1. Mix together cream cheese, horseradish, lemon juice, Tabasco, and Worcestershire sauce together until smooth.//

2. Fold in onion and crab.

3. Pour into baking dish and bake for 30 minutes in a 350-degree oven.

Chili Dip

Prep Time	1 min.
Cook Time	5 mins.
Serving Size	¼ cup
Calories	83.1
Carbs	5 g
Fat	6.3 g
Protein	2.2 g

Ingredients

- 8 oz. light sour cream

- 1 tbsp. chili powder

- ½ tsp. salt

- 2 tbsp. chopped cilantro

Let's Cook:

1. Place all ingredients into a bowl and whisk together with a wire whisk or large fork.

2. Place in refrigerator and allow to chill for best results.

BLT Dip

Prep Time	15 mins.
Cook Time	0 mins.
Serving Size	1/8 cup
Calories	92.4
Carbs	2.7 g
Fat	8.2 g
Protein	2.2 g

Ingredients

- 1 c. sour cream
- ¼ c. mayonnaise
- ½ c. crumbled bacon
- 1 tbsp. chives
- 1 ½ c. shredded romaine lettuce
- ½ c. chopped roma tomatoes

Let's Cook:

1. Mix together first four ingredients in a medium mixing bowl.

2. Layer lettuce on the bottom of a casserole dish.

3. Spread sour cream mixture over lettuce.

4. Place tomatoes on top and chill in the refrigerator for about 1 hour.

Caramelized Sweet Onion Dip

Prep Time	30 mins.
Cook Time	0 mins.
Serving Size	¼ cup
Calories	54.5
Carbs	2.4 g
Fat	4.8 g
Protein	0.8 g

Ingredients

- 2 tbsp. olive oil

- 2 sweet onions

- 1 c. sour cream

- ½ c. buttermilk

- 1 tsp. salt

Let's Cook:

1. Cut onions in half and thinly slice each onion.

2. Heat olive oil in a nonstick pan over medium heat and add onions. Cook for about 20 minutes.

Onions will be done when they are brown, sticky, and caramelized.

3. Place onions in a bowl and allow to chill for 1 hour.

4. Pulse onions in a food process along with the remaining ingredients until just combined.

5. Transfer to serving bowl and chill for an additional hour before serving.

Best Practices & Common Mistakes

Do's

Store dips properly

One of the most important things in regards to food is food safety. Most people make party dips ahead of time, as they are quick and easy to make ahead of time. Plus many dips need time to sit to allow the flavors to meld together. If you make the dips ahead of time, make sure you are storing them properly, so as not to compromise food safety. Cold dips need to be stored in the fridge until time. Warm dips should also be kept warm until ready to serve.

Transport dip safely

Transportation is another key element to party dips. Transporting them improperly can result in disaster when you get to your final destination. Creamy dips can be safely transported in plastic baggies and then transferred to serving bowls when you arrive. Layered dips should be transported in dishes that have tight fitting lids. Cold dips should be transported in insulated coolers with ice packs. Warm dips can be transported in insulated coolers to help keep them warm.

Pick the right dip

What dip you make is really going to depend on the occasion. For example, if it is during the summer you don't necessarily want to make a hot dip. Summer parties are often outdoors and cool and creamy dips work best for those occasions. Warm dips are best kept for indoor parties during the cooler months. And, always think about colors when presenting your dips because the better they look the more in demand they will be.

Don'ts

Choose the wrong dippers

What you serve with your dip is going to make a big difference in how well your dip goes over. For example, if you are serving vegetables as your dippers you don't want to make a hot dip. You want to serve a creamy, cool style dip, such as a dill dip. Chips, crackers, and toast make great dippers for hot dips, as well as several cold dips.

Make the dip too early

Timing is everything when it comes to dips. If you make a hot dip too early and keep it warm in the Crockpot you still run the risk of overheating it. Crockpots on the warm setting can help keep foods warm, but they can also overcook the edges giving our dip a crunchy texture instead of smooth. Leaving some dips in the refrigerator for too long can affect the overall texture of the dip. Some dips will end up with soggy ingredients others will lose their correct taste. The key is to make the dip just enough ahead of time to allow the flavors to meld into each other, not to overpower one another.

Make the dips too spicy

When making dips for a party you need to take the entire crowd into account. You might like a lot of spice, but not everybody does. Some dips are meant to be spicy, which is fine. If making a spicy dip don't increase the spiciness, unless you know the majority of the people you are serving will eat it that hot. Sticking with mild is usually your best option when making dips for large groups that you are not familiar with.

Conclusion

I hope that you enjoyed reading this recipe book, as much as I enjoyed writing it. In reading this book I hope you have come to the realization that there is a lot more thought that goes into making the perfect party dip then most people realize. Making the perfect party dip means you need to pick the right dip for the occasion, but it also means you need to pick the right dippers to serve with it. After all, the sign of a perfect dip is one that is gone before the party even gets started.

Perhaps the greatest thing that I discovered while writing this book was that I did not have to give up my healthy lifestyle to enjoy parties anymore. I was able to learn how to make healthy party dips that fit with my new lifestyle choice. Even better is the fact that these dips do not lack flavor despite the fact that they are considered to be low carb. Even the sweet dessert style dips are made to fit my low carb lifestyle, plus none of my friends who are anti-low carb even realize these dips are made differently than their full carb counterparts.

So, now that you know how easy it is to make the perfect party dips, all you have to do is get started planning your next party!

Bonus: Your FREE Gift

As a token of our appreciation, please take advantage of the **FREE Gift** - a lifetime **VIP Membership** at our book club.

Follow the link below to download your FREE books:

http://bit.ly/vipbookclub

As a VIP member, you will get an instant **FREE** access to exclusive new releases and bestselling books.

Printed in Great Britain
by Amazon